AF444833

# A New Rubáiyát of Omar Khayyám

## Age-old Wisdom for a 21$^{st}$ Century World

by Jay Ter Louw

A New Rubáiyát of Omar Khayyám

Age-old Wisdom for a 21st Century World
© 2020 Jay Ter Louw
All Rights Reserved


A New Rubáiyát of Omar Khayyám is the original work of Jay Ter Louw,
published in 2020 through Kindle Direct Publishing.


The original text of the Rubáiyát of Omar Khayyám is included.
Originally published in 1859, this portion is in the public domain.


**ISBN:** 9798647553706


Companion material available at: anewrubaiyat.com

Front cover image by Nik Niklz licensed through Shutterstock.com

Nightingale by Ollga P (page 11) licensed through Shutterstock.com

Ptolemaic Spheres illustration (page 24) licensed through Alamy.com

*For Jancie,*
*the love of my life,*
*who introduced me to the*
*Rubáiyát in 1969*

# CONTENTS

# Preface

Do you have a keepsake you have treasured for more than 50 years, other than, perhaps, a wedding ring?

In the springtime of my youth, between the Ides of March and graduation in June 1969, I was falling head-over-heels in love. My high school sweetheart gave me a gift copy of the Rubáiyát of Omar Khayyám, originally translated into English and published by Edward Fitzgerald more than 100 years before. A couple of the verses were circled for my notice, including:

> Here with a Loaf of Bread beneath the Bough,
> A Flask of Wine, a Book of Verse—and Thou
> Beside me singing in the Wilderness—
> And Wilderness is paradise enow.

I was caught by the exotic imagery of the opening verse, the Morning putting stars to flight with a slingshot stone, catching the Sultan's turret in a noose of light. So many verses were full of pithy wisdom that rivals Bible proverbs and parables, and a melodic language reminiscent of Shakespeare.

For those new to the Rubáiyát Omar Khayyám, the supposed author, lived around 1048—1131. Fitzgerald called him "the Tentmaker." Omar was likely an astronomer and certainly a poet, but there are still debates about attribution of this poetry. Taken at face value, he was impious and blatant in his disregard for much religious dogma but showed in his verses a deep understanding of the human spirit and the extent of our yearning for purpose in life and death.

As a lay minister, I came to use this book as a resource for weddings and funerals, especially for people with an unclear or ecumenical faith. The truths expressed in the Rubáiyát stand by themselves, and there are few that engender disagreement. Even those are often couched as self-confessed weaknesses of Khayyám.

When I was young, I did not like to spend much time reading. There were too many things I wanted to do and later, too many things I had to do. So, I developed an appreciation for short works, and things you did not have to spend much time figuring out. I particularly liked the poems of Stephen Crane, the ninth surviving child of a Methodist-Episcopal minister. His poems were short, pointed, irreligious and easy to understand most of the time. I found the same quality in the Rubáiyát.

But there were a few of the verses that were obscure, and I wrestled with them. Though I understood more and more as years went by, I wondered if others had the same struggle, not only with the words, but with the allusions. They were written for a twelfth-century Persian and loosely translated for a nineteenth-century Englishman. Our modern influences include the major works of literature, but also the news, movies, television, and music—the Rubáiyát of Omar Khayyám needed an update.

The work before you is my effort to accomplish that goal. I don't want you to lose the magic of the original, so the poetry is compared verse-by-verse. The objective was not to create a more accurate translation, but from the first edition of Fitzgerald to paraphrase the spirit and overall message of each verse and the work as a whole, with reference to a more modern experience and mindset.

For each verse, my new "translation" will be on top, and Fitzgerald's original will appear below.

At the end I have added some notes that may help with the historic and modern allusions and provide some resources if you would like to dig a little deeper.

Old Khayyám would suggest that you read these verses with help from a glass of wine or a gin and tonic, or at least a spirit of expectation. The Caravan is setting off, and we don't want to leave without you.


Jay Ter Louw

1

Wake up! The sudden breaking of the day
has scurried the lingering stars away.
And every hopeful moment shines on you
with rays of joy or sorrow, come what may.

عمر خيام

Awake! For Morning in the Bowl of Night

has flung the Stone that puts the Stars to Flight:

And Lo! The Hunter of the East has caught

The Sultan's Turret in a Noose of Light.

2

And I woke from a vivid dream, no doubt,
where I'd heard the bartender give a shout,
"Last call, everyone. Fill your glasses
before the magic whiskey all runs out."

عمر خيام

Dreaming when Dawn's Left hand was in the Sky

I heard a Voice within the tavern cry,

"Awake, my Little ones, and fill the Cup

Before Life's Liquor in its Cup be dry."

3

So, I went early, no waiting to pack,
to the tavern door with a neon plaque:
"You really can leave any time you want,
but once you go, you can never come back."

عمر خیام

And, as the Cock crew, those who stood before

The Tavern shouted— "Open then the Door!

You know how little while we have to stay,

And, once departed, may return no more."

4

With the Breath of Life early spring comes 'round.
Consider this gem of wisdom I found:
A Young man's fancy turns to thoughts of love;
A tender crocus springs up from the ground.

عمر خیام

Now the New Year reviving old Desires,

The thoughtful Soul to Solitude retires,

Where the White Hand Of Moses on the Bough

Puts out, and Jesus from the Ground suspires.

5

The Ancient Wonders now all decompose;
once fertile fields are overrun by crows.
Babylon's glory song withered to tears,
but still by the river a garden grows.

عمر خيام

Iram indeed is gone with all its Rose

And Jamshýd's Sev'n-ring'd Cup

    where no one knows;

But still the Vine her ancient Ruby yields,

And still a Garden by the Water blows.


6

"The Rose must be crimson," my True Love said.
But all I could find were sallow instead.
A song all night from a thicket of thorns,
left one red rose where the Nightingale bled.

عمر خيام

And David's Lips are lock't; but in divine

High piping Pehlevi, with "Wine! Wine! Wine!

Red Wine!"—the Nightingale cries to the Rose

That yellow Cheek of hers to incarnadine.

The legend says that all Roses were once pale.  In Oscar Wilde's version (1888), the Nightingale knows the young man needs a red one to win the girl's heart.  The bird seeks a rosebush and sings all night, thorns piercing his breast, and leaving a single red Rose.

Image by Ollga P, licensed through Shutterstock.com

7

So, pour a decanter of wine to quaff
and give the worries of winter a scoff.
This journey of life won't last very long;
the Caravan has already set off.

عمر خيام

Come, fill the Cup, and in the Fire of Spring
The Winter Garment of Repentance fling:
The Bird of Time has but a little way
To fly—and Lo! The Bird is on the Wing.


8

A thousand blossoms with the sun did flirt,
a thousand more to the earth did revert.
This was a time for lovers and heroes;
my favorites were buried beneath the dirt.

عمر خيام

And look a thousand blossoms with the day
Woke—and a thousand scatter's into clay:
And this first Summer Month that brings the Rose
Shall take Jamshýd and Kaikobád away.

9

Khayyám the agèd has stories to tell—
ponder life's mystery under his spell.
Forget your trivial daily concerns.
Don't even listen for the dinner bell!

عمر خيام

But come with old Khayyám, and leave the Lot
Of Kaikobád and Kaikhosrú forgot:
Let Rustum lay about him as he will,
Or Hátim cry Supper—heed them not.


10

Come find with me some idle tract of land,
between sweet gardens and hot desert sand.
Who cares if you're King, or just a hired hand?
In fact, pity the rank's heavy demand.

عمر خيام

With me along some Strip of Herbage strown
That just divides the desert from the sown,
Where name of Slave and Sultán scarce is known,
And pity Sultán Mahmud on his Throne.

11

Let's break some bread beneath a shady tree,
open wine and a book of poetry.
If you are here, even in a desert,
the wilderness is paradise to me.

عمر خیام

Here with a Loaf of Bread beneath the Bough,
A Flask of Wine, a Book of Verse—and Thou
Beside me singing in the Wilderness—
And Wilderness is Paradise enow.

12

How pleasant now to dwell upon this earth;
others think that heaven holds far more worth.
A bird in hand is worth two in the bush—
let that be your spiritual rebirth.

عمر خیام

"How sweet is mortal Sovranty!"—think some:
Others— "How blest the Paradise to come!"
Ah, take the Cash in hand and waive the Rest;
Oh, the brave Music of a *distant* Drum!

14

## 13

Watch the quick puff of dandelion weeds;
laughing they blow wherever the wind leads.
Our beauty is not how pretty we are—
the garden's lasting value are the seeds.

عمر خیام

Look to the Rose that blows about us—"Lo,

Laughing," she says, "into the World I blow:

At once the silken Tassel of my Purse

Tear, and its Treasure on the Garden throw."


## 14

We keep on working, but stay in arrears,
or maybe we're stars, and everyone cheers.
Success or failure, what does it matter?
Say, where will you be in a hundred years?

عمر خیام

The Worldly Hope men set their Hearts upon

Turns Ashes—or it prospers; and anon,

Like Snow upon the Desert's dusty face

Lighting a little Hour or two—is gone.

15

We honor farmers who plant golden grain,
and tender its growing through sun and rain.
We plant farmers, too, without any gold.
Let us exhume them and re-live the pain.

عمر خيام

And those who husbanded the Golden Grain,

And those who flung it to the Winds like Rain,

Alike to no such aureate Earth are turn'd

As, buried once, Men want dug up again.

16

Think how our life is like a circus show:
out of the darkness, see the spotlight glow!
Star after star takes the stage to applause,
and taking a final bow, off they go.

عمر خيام

Think, in this batter'd Caravanserai

Whose Doorways are alternate Night and Day,

How Sultán after Sultán with his Pomp

Abode his hour or two, and went his way.

## 17

The Taj Mahal is now a travel scam,
its famous splendor hardly more than sham.
The princes, with their pomp and circumstance
now rest in tombs just like the Old Khayyám.

عمر خیام

They say the Lion and the Lizard keep
The Courts where Jamshýd gloried and drank deep;
And Bahrám, that great hunter—the Wild Ass
Stamps over his Head, and he lies fast asleep.


## 18

Roses are red, and violets are blue.
The graveyard bestows more intense a hue—
as if from blood of buried kings and saints
a secret fountain pushes color through.

عمر خیام

I sometimes think that never blows so red

The Rose as where some buried Cæsar bled;

That every Hyacinth the Garden wears

Dropt in its lap from some once lovely head.

# 19

Tread lightly as you walk across the lawn—
the blades of grass from tender earth are drawn,
all nourished by the remnants decomposed
of once vital beings, now dead and gone.

عمر خيام

And this delightful herb whose tender Green
Fledges the River's Lip on which we lean—
Ah, lean upon it lightly! For who knows
From what once lovely Lip it springs unseen.


# 20

Oh, My Love, Drink away your angst and pain—
the future fears that drive you half insane.
We may become a whole new universe;
maybe we'll be a single drop of rain.

عمر خيام

Oh, my Belovéd, fill the Cup that clears
To-Day of past regrets and future Fears—
To-morrow? —Why Tomorrow I may be
Myself with Yesterday's Sev'n Thousand Years.

21

Pull away from the crowd and drink a toast—
you follow footsteps of a countless host
who drank before you and will drink after.
But, remember the one you loved the most.

عمر خيام

Lo! Some we loved, the loveliest and best

That Time and fate of all their Vintage prest,

Have drunk their Cup a Round or two before,

And one by one crept silently to Rest.


22

In summer, we make merry mid the flowers
where predecessors whiled away the hours.
We stand or sit on the shoulders of giants.
When we take our leave, who will stand on ours?

عمر خيام

And we, that now make merry in the Room

They left, and Summer dresses in new Bloom.

Ourselves must we beneath the Couch of Earth

Descend, ourselves to make a Couch—for whom?

## 23

Enjoy the most of every good endeavor,
before the reaper comes your soul to sever:
Ashes to ashes, dust to dust you turn—
no wine, no song, and silence lasts forever.

عمر خيام

Ah, make the most of what we yet may spend.

Before we too into the Dust descend;

Dust into Dust, and under Dust, to lie,

Sans Wine, sans Song, sans Singer, and—sans End!

## 24

To those who save up for tomorrow's pleasure,
and those today who carefully do measure,
a warning sounds from a dark, distant tower:
"O Fools! You cannot count on any treasure."

عمر خيام

Alike for those who for To-Day prepare,

And those that after a To-Morrow stare,

A Muezzin from the Tower of Darkness cries

"Fools! Your Reward is neither Here nor There!"

## 25

Preachers and pundits do pontificate
on the world to come and the world of late.
Their foolish words rile us up like a storm,
but eventually they dissipate.

عمر خیام

Why, all the Saints and Sages who discuss'd
Of the Two Worlds so learnedly, are thrust
Like foolish Prophets forth; their Words to Scorn
Are scatter'd, and their Mouths are filled with Dust.


## 26

So, while the sterile debate wanes and waxes,
come sit a while where Old Khayyam relaxes.
Life flies too fast for redundant disputing—
the only things certain are death and taxes.

عمر خیام

Oh, come with old Khayyám, and leave the Wise
To talk; one thing is certain, that Life flies;
One thing is certain, and the Rest is Lies;
The Flower that once has blown for ever dies.

27

Since my early days, every place I've been
I asked the wisest, but to my chagrin
the saints and scholars argued back and forth;
leaving, I knew less than when I came in.

عمر خيام

Myself when young did eagerly frequent

Doctor and Saint, and heard great Argument

About it and about: but evermore

Came out by the same Door as in I went.


28

I learned from the wise how to take a stand;
the art of debate was at my command.
I crafted my arguments block-by-block,
but the starting premise was shifting sand.

عمر خيام

With them the Seed of Wisdom did I sow,

And with my own hand labour'd it to grow:

And this was all the Harvest that I reap'd—

I came like Water, and like the Wind I go.

29

Perhaps you need another metaphor:
We thought these issues were a vital core.
Our lofty thoughts transfixing the air, were
hot wind blowing through a revolving door.

عمر خیام

Into this Universe, and *why* not knowing,
Nor *whence*, like Water willy-nilly flowing:
And out of it, as Wind along the Waste,
I know not *whither*, willy-nilly blowing.


30

We disputed questions until we burst;
we ask what's on second, say Who's on first.
The talk becomes a comedy routine;
I need another drink to quench my thirst.

عمر خیام

What, without asking, hither hurried *whence*?
And without asking, *whither* hurried hence!
Another and another Cup to drown
The Memory of this Impertinence!

Khayyám was an astronomer and understood Saturn to be in the seventh sphere based on its movements relative to sun and other planets. "Up from Earth's Center through the Seventh Gate …"

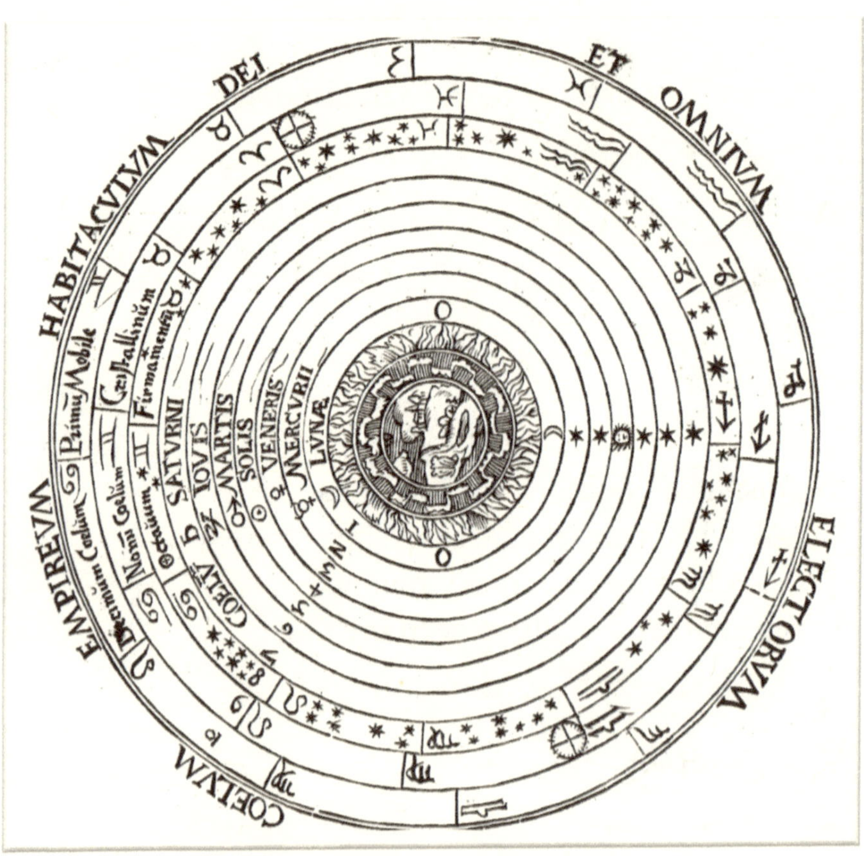



Geocentric system of the universe embraced by Ptolemy, showing the earth at the center, with sun, moon, fixed planets and stars based on their perceived sphere of rotation.

From "Cosmographia" by Peter Apian (Antwerp, 1539) Woodcut. Imaged licensed through alamy.com

## 31

To explore the cosmos, I boldly traveled.
Some highways were paved,
    and some paths just graveled.
I never found out how fate is determined—
the mystery of death remains unraveled.

عمر خيام

Up from Earth's Centre through the Seventh Gate

I rose, and on the Throne of Saturn sate,

And many Knots unravel'd by the Road;

But not the Knot of Human Death and Fate.


## 32

Some plans were good but failed in execution.
The best sacrifice gave no absolution.
The talk of perfect harmony fell still—
not every puzzle has a good solution.

عمر خيام

There was a Door to which I found no Key:

There was a Veil past which I could not see:

Some little Talk awhile of Me and Thee

There seem'd—and then no more of Thee and Me.

33

I asked God Himself for a lamp to guide
us little children that on earth abide.
"What should we do, stumbling here in the dark?"
"Just close your eyes and trust Me," he replied.

عمر خيام

Then to the rolling Heav'n itself I cried,

Asking, "What Lamp had Destiny to guide

Her little Children stumbling in the Dark?"

And— "A blind Understanding!" Heav'n replied.


34

So, I turned to the cup of wine instead,
asking for guidance. Here is what she said:
"Listen—your lip to my lip, hold me close.
Drink me now! There's no drinking when you're dead."

عمر خيام

Then to this earthen Bowl did I adjourn

My Lip the secret Well of Life to learn:

And Lip to Lip it murmur'd— "While you live

Drink! —for once dead you never shall return."

35

I imagine the cup of wine alive—
that with magic powers can she connive
to cause remembrance and effect forgets,
and with her kisses I might thrive.

عمر خيام

I think the Vessel, that with fugitive

Articulation answer'd, once did live,

And merry-make; and the cold Lip I kiss'd

How many Kisses might it take—and give!

36

One evening, a busy Potter I found
thumping raw clay. He'd pound and pound and pound!
The clay spoke up, although his "tongue" was smashed,
"Please, a little gentler next time around?"

عمر خيام

For in the Market-place, one Dusk of Day,

I watch'd the Potter thumping his wet Clay:

And with its all obliterated Tongue

It murmur'd— "Gently, Brother, gently pray!"

37

Yesterday abandoned me in a huff,
Tomorrow is imaginary fluff.
So pour us all another toasting round,
"To Today! It will have to be enough."

عمر خیام

Ah, fill the Cup: —what boots it to repeat
How Time is slipping underneath our Feet:
Unborn To-Morrow, and dead Yesterday,
Why fret about them if To-Day be sweet!

38

We have but one moment for life's endeavor—
a single minute to savor whatever.
There's no time for us; there's no place for us.
Anyway, who does want to live forever?

عمر خیام

One Moment in Annihilation's Waste,
One Moment, of the Well of Life to taste—
The Stars are setting and the Caravan
Starts for the Dawn of Nothing—Oh, make haste!

## 39

We chase a chosen cause for years and years.
When we reach the end and the smoke all clears,
should we have smelled a few more of the roses,
not wasting time on disappointment's tears?

عمر خيام

How long, how long, in infinite Pursuit

Of This and That endeavor and dispute?

Better be merry with the fruitful Grape

Than sadden after none, or bitter, Fruit.


## 40

You should consider a change in your life
from nagging old reason that brings such strife.
You may find your bed happier if you
take the grape's daughter to be your new wife.

عمر خيام

You know, my Friends, how long since in my House

For a new Marriage I did make Carouse:

Divorced old barren Reason from my Bed,

And took the Daughter of the Vine to Spouse.

## 41

We climb to Everest's exalted height
and expect the scene to be black and white.
Alas, from high we find the landscape gray;
the wineglass gives similar, softer light.

عمر خیام

For "Is" and "Is-Not" though *with* Rule and Line,

And "Up-and-Down" *without* I could define,

I yet in all only cared to know,

Was never deep in anything but—Wine.


## 42

I stood at the tavern door and looked in
at tables where the discussions had been.
The angry debaters faded away.
It's all different on tonic and gin.

عمر خیام

And lately, by the Tavern Door agape,

Came stealing through the Dusk an Angel Shape

Bearing a Vessel on his Shoulder; and

He bid me taste of it; and 'twas—the Grape!

# 43

The arguments filled the tavern with chatter.
Some pushed the former and some pressed the latter
religious and political beliefs.
Enough alcohol, and the points don't matter.

عمر خیام

The Grape that can with Logic absolute

The Two-and-Seventy jarring Sects confute:

The subtle Alchemist that in a Trice

Life's leaden Metal into Gold transmute.


# 44

There is a bleak force, an evil dark side
with minions of scoundrels standing allied—
this Dementor deploys soul-wrenching power
to cause rampant devastation world-wide.

عمر خیام

The mighty Mahmud, the victorious Lord,

That all the misbelieving and black Horde

Of Fears and Sorrows that infest the Soul

Scatters and slays with his enchanted Sword.

# 45

So, God has filled the universe with rules
and discordant quarrels beset the schools.
I am a solitary simpleton,
and it's not fine for God to menace fools.

عمر خيام

But leave the Wise to wrangle, and with me

The quarrel of the universe let be:

And, in some corner of the Hubbub coucht,

Make Game of that which makes as much of Thee.


# 46

Life's movie frames flitter by one by one—
we are just a filmstrip cleverly done:
The screen an old bedsheet hung in the yard;
the brilliant projector bulb is the sun.

عمر خيام

For in and out, above, about, below,

'Tis nothing but a Magic Shadow-show,

Play'd in a Box whose Candle is the Sun,

Round which we Phantom Figures come and go.

47

At last call, what will be your legacy;
with what stamp will you mark eternity?
When you cash out, whatever you have been,
whatever you are, you will always be.

عمر خیام

And if the Wine you drink, the Lip you press,
End in the Nothing all Things end in —Yes—
Then fancy while Thou art, Thou art but what
Thou shalt be - Nothing - Thou shalt not be less.


48

A table for two Old Khayyám has laid.
Come, sit a while until the shadows fade.
The time will soon come for that darker draught.
Drink that liquor, too. Do not be afraid.

عمر خیام

While the Rose blows along the River Brink,
With old Khayyám the Ruby Vintage drink:
And when the Angel with his darker Draught
Draws up to Thee—take that, and do not shrink.

## 49

The chess board is made of black and white blocks,
like nights and days are marked on your clocks.
The Master plays you—Queens, Bishops and Pawns,
and when He's done, puts you back in the box.

عمر خيام

'Tis all a Chequer-board of Nights and Days

Where Destiny with Men for Pieces plays:

Hither and thither moves, and mates, and slays.

And one by one back in the Closet lays.

## 50

In the arena, see how the ball goes;
fast or slow, where it stops, nobody knows.
With curve or spin, it can look like magic.
Your path is controlled by the One who throws.

عمر خيام

The Ball no question makes of Ayes and Noes,

But Right or Left as strikes the Player goes;

And He that toss'd Thee down into the Field,

He knows about it all—He knows—HE knows.

34

51

The sentence spoken cannot be unheard;
hit "send" and it flies like an uncaged bird.
However sorry or smart you may be,
it will never erase a single word.

عمر خیام

The Moving Finger writes; and, having writ,
Moves on; nor all thy Piety nor Wit
Shall lure it back to cancel half a Line,
nor all thy Tears wash out a Word of it.


52

We all chase for wisdom under this dome—
sky, earth, and heaven—wherever we roam,
without much more insight, I fear. There are
no better answers than we find at home.

عمر خیام

And that inverted Bowl we call the Sky,
Whereunder crawling coopt we live and die,
Lift not thy hands to *It* for help—for It
Rolls impotently on as Thou or I.

## 53

They say God fashioned the first man from clay;
our humble substance never goes away.
The story He penned upon creation
is the same tale He reads on judgement day.

عمر خیام

With Earth's first Clay They did the Last man knead,

And then of the last harvest sow'd the Seed:

Yea, the first Morning of Creation wrote

What the last Dawn of Reckoning shall read.


## 54

In the circle of life, we find our birth—
a blazing star-place established our worth.
You are a gear in the cosmic clockwork—
transcendent purpose mirrored here on earth.

عمر خیام

I tell Thee this—When, starting from the Goal,

Over the Shoulders of the flaming Foal

Of Heav'n Parwin and Mushtara they flung,

In my predestin'd Plot of Dust and Soul.

## 55

Maybe you're golden, perhaps I'm a blank.
They think you're a genius, I'm just a crank.
But I'll do the laughing, when they one day
from me make the key that unlocks the bank.

عمر خیام

The Vine had struck a Fibre; which about

If clings my Being—Let the Sufi flout;

Of my base Metal may be filed a Key,

That shall unlock the Door he howls without.

## 56

One thing I know, and certain to be right:
More likely than in a cathedral bright,
in a dark, dusty tavern I might find
a spark of love or truth for just one night.

عمر خیام

And this I know; whether the one True Light,

Kindle to Love, or Wrath—consume me quite,

One glimpse of It within the Tavern caught

Better than in the Temple lost outright.

## 57

And if I falter in life's sorry path,
though I am ready to endure God's wrath,
with predestination and circumstance
the fault can't be only mine. Do the math!

عمر خيام

Oh Thou, who didst with Pitfall and with Gin

Beset the Road I was to wander in,

Thou wilt not with Predestination round

Enmesh me, and impute my Fall to Sin.


## 58

Acknowledge God's sovereignty over all,
Who crafted first man and allowed his fall.
He weighs in the balance all that we do;
the sentence: The writing is on the wall.

عمر خيام

Oh, Thou, who Man of baser Earth didst make,

And who with Eden didst devise the Snake;

For all the Sin wherewith the face of man

Is blacken'd, man's Forgiveness give—and take!

One Ramadan morning as day was breaking,
the various pots of the craftsman's making
arrayed on shelves in the pottery shop
as if from a deep sleep began awaking.

عمر خيام

KUZA-NAMA

Listen again. One evening at the close
Of Ramazán, ere the better Moon arose,
In that old Potter's Shop I stood alone
With the clay Population round in Rows.

60

I watched a little while, and then I caught
that some pots could talk (though many could not).
A wee impertinent teacup spoke up,
"Say, who's the Potter, and who is the pot?"

عمر خيام

And, strange to tell, among the Earthen Lot
Some could articulate, while others not:
And suddenly one more impatient cried—
"Who *is* the Potter, pray, and who the Pot?"

# 61

Said one, "It took the Potter time to make me,
to turn and mold and decorate and bake me.
It's unlikely after all that hard effort
He would now want to cast away and break me."

عمر خیام

Then said another— "Surely not in vain
My substance from the common Earth was ta'en,
That He who subtly wrought me into Shape
Should stamp me back to common Earth again."


# 62

Another added, "You know, that is true.
And after all He and I have been through—
we've eaten and drunk and toasted together—
It would be hard for him to bid adieu."

عمر خیام

Another said— "Why, ne'er a peevish Boy
Would break the Bowl from which he drank in Joy;
Shall He that *made* the Vessel in pure Love
And Fancy, in an after Rage destroy?"

63

"I'm not in His good graces, I can tell.
My ugly handle is bent all to hell,"
a misshapen pitcher hurried to add,
"His fault! He didn't make me quite as well."

عمر خيام

None answer'd this; but after Silence spake
A Vessel of a more ungainly make:
"They sneer at me for leaning all awry;
What! Did the hand of the Potter shake?"


64

"Some talk of a savage, end-of-world judge
who from a scale of perfection won't budge.
But don't worry, mates, I know this good fellow;
at the end of life He won't hold a grudge."

عمر خيام

Said one— "Folks of a surly Tapster tell,
And daub his Visage with the Smoke of Hell;
They talk of some strict Testing of us — Pish !
He's a Good Fellow, and 'twill all be well."

## 65

Another of the pots sighed deep and said,
"I've gotten so dry, I think I'm half dead.
Please pour a few drops of wine into me
and I'll make my way to the light ahead."

عمر خیام

Then said another with a long-drawn Sigh,
"My Clay with long oblivion is gone dry:
But, fill me with the old familiar Juice,
Methinks I might recover by-and-bye!"


## 66

As nighttime came, the conversation slowed;
the ending crescent of Ramadan showed.
The vessels all jumped in expectant joy
as they heard the wild Champagne cork explode.

عمر خیام

So while the Vessels one by one were speaking,
One spied the little Crescent all were seeking:
And then they jogg'd each other, "Brother! Brother!
Hark to the Porter's Shoulder-knot a creaking."

(THIS ENDS THE BOOK OF POTS)

67

When eventide comes and my life's complete,
tenderly wrap me with a winding sheet.
Bury me simply in a peaceful meadow
with a jug of punch at my head and feet.

عمر خيام

Ah, with the Grape my fading Life provide,

And wash my Body whence the Life has died,

And in a Windingsheet of Vine-leaf wrapt,

So bury me by some sweet Garden side.


68

Though my ashes rest in a hidden lair,
a sweet perfume will come from who knows where
that brings a surprise smile to passersby
as the fragrance catches them unaware.

عمر خيام

That ev'n my buried Ashes such a Snare

Of Perfume shall fling up into the Air,

As not a True Believer passing by

But shall be overtaken unaware.

## 69

This cup of wine it's my habit to clutch
is thought by many to be just a crutch.
For me, it's a means of fresh transformation;
my detractors complain I drink too much.

عمر خیام

Indeed the Idols I have loved so long

Have done my Credit in Men's Eye much wrong:

Have drown'd my Honour in a shallow Cup,

And sold my Reputation for a Song.


## 70

I often did something not what I meant—
my Mardi Gras often came *after* lent!
The better-than-thou feeling I achieved
oft made me sorry that I did repent.

عمر خیام

Indeed, indeed, Repentance oft before

I swore—but was I sober when I swore?

And then and then came Spring, and Rose-in-hand

My thread-bare Penitence apieces tore.

71

Though many disparage the altered state,
and the tavern's vile company berate,
true to the legacy as I write here,
the spirit and spirits helped me create.

عمر خیام

And much as Wine has play'd the Infidel,

And robb'd me of my Robe of Honour—well,

I often wonder what the Vintners buy

One half sop precious as the Goods they sell.


72

Spring disappears in the blink of an eye;
the ink and the wineglass both have run dry.
The song nears crescendo, then fades away.
Time and the Nightingale both had to fly.

عمر خیام

Alas, that Spring should vanish with the Rose!

That Youth's sweet-scented Manuscript should close!

The Nightingale that in the Branches sang,

Ah, whence, and whither flown again, who knows!

73

And, My Love, with you and fate I'd conspire
to throw all the bad things onto the fire,
redo our mistakes and relive our joys—
make everything more like our hearts' desire.

عمر خیام

Ah Love! Could thou and I with fate conspire

To grasp this sorry Scheme of Things entire,

Would not we shatter it to bits—and then

Re-mould it nearer to the Heart's Desire!


74

You are the Love of My Life, and whether
the threads of our lives can keep their tether
or be blown off at the rise of the moon,
I'm yours, here in the garden forever.

عمر خیام

Ah, Moon of my Delight who know'st no wane,

The Moon of Heav'n is rising once again:

How oft hereafter rising shall she look

Through this same Garden after me—in vain!

remembered Zion." (NKJV). A Rastafari song, *By the Rivers of Babylon*, came out around 1978.

Verse 6: There is a long association with the rose and the nightingale in Persian poetry, and Oscar Wilde wrote a short story, *The Nightingale and the Rose*. In both, the upshot of the story is that roses used to be only yellow or pale, but through the sacrificial song of a nightingale as it was being pierced by the thorns of the rose, it became red. I also saw a tie to the song, Scarlet Ribbons, written by Jack Segal (lyrics) and Evelyn Danzig in 1949. The version I like was recorded by Willie Nelson.

Verse 7: In the original, the Caravan shows up in verses 16 and 38.

Verse 8: Jamshýd  and Kaikobád were Persian kings.

Verse 9: Kaikhosrú was another Persian King, Rustum was a great hero, and Hátim Tai was known for his hospitality.

Verse 10: Sultan Mahmud of Ghazni ruled in Afghanistan 998 – 1030 AD.

Verse 11: This was the first verse Jancie had circled for me. We did a picnic one day by a small local river. Though under age, I carried a bottle of wine in my work toolbox, but we had to open it with a screwdriver.

Verse 12: Whether you believe in the theology of this verse or not, we should savor *this* life, and endeavor to do right in *this* world, regardless of the possible implications to our eternal destiny.

Verse 13: The purse is the Rose's stamen. To me, the image of blowing a dandelion into the wind and watching the seeds scatter was especially vivid.

Verse 14: The philosophy presented here could make life seem pointless, but refer to verse 47 for a more optimistic view.

Verse 15:  The original may refer in some way to martyrs and relics, and our desire to dig up the bones for worship or for our museums. We also tend to re-write history as our sensibilities change.

Verse 16: Night and Day shows up again in the checker board (verse 49).

Verse 17: Many of the ancient garden cities had become abandoned ruins, overrun by wild animals. Bahram V is famous in Iranian history, ruling 420 – 438 AD. Old palaces now are less likely to be totally abandoned as the world is more crowded and history has become better documented. Instead of ruins, they become tourist attractions. But their glory is hollow—the sultans and kings are still dead. Khayyám is buried in Nishapur in his own garden, which is now a tourist attraction.

Verse 18: The modern "Roses are red" kindergarten poem sounds trite, but children's verses often seed a deeper meaning. There are many allusions in history to flowers blooming from the blood of the slain, and most every cemetery is marked with flowers.

Verse 19: The river's lip is its bank where we sit.

Verse 20: The Highwaymen were Kris Kristofferson, Johnny Cash, Waylon Jennings, and Willie Nelson, recording their famous album in 1985. On the first track, Johnny Cash sings: "I fly a starship across the Universe divide. And when I reach the other side, I'll find a place to rest my spirit if I can. Perhaps I may become a highwayman again. Or I may simply be a single drop of rain. But I will remain. And I'll be back again and again and again."

Verse 21: The Whiskey Bards, a singing group from Arizona, say "It's not the whiskey, it is the company."

Verse 22: "On the Shoulders of Giants" is an ancient gem, dating back to the 12th Century's, Bernard of Chartres, or even earlier. Now it is commonplace, appearing as the title in Stephen Hawking's compilation of the works Copernicus, Galileo, Kepler, Newton, and Einstein, and in hundreds of other places as well.

Verse 23: The original is similar to Shakespeare's *As You Like It*, Act II, Scene VII.

Verse 24: The Muezzin is the man who chants loudly from the top of the minaret, calling the faithful to prayer.

Verse 25: In *The Name of the Rose*, Umberto Eco really nails the lengths to which men will go in arguing the minutiae of theology.  I learned it growing up in the defense of Presbyterian beliefs against the Baptists in the 1960s and against the Pentecostals in the 1980s. Let's not start on the political polarization that engenders so much strife. Unfortunately, though the particular topics dissipate, the spirit of argument often doesn't.

Verse 26: Though the saying was around earlier, Benjamin Franklin made the quote famous for us: "Our new Constitution is established, and has the appearance that promises permanency; but in this world nothing can be said to be certain, except death and taxes."

Verse 27: While it is true there are two sides to any issue, the more pertinent question is whether you have to take sides at all.

Verse 28: I was a debater in college and learned to argue both sides of any issue. But I find as I grow older, I know less now than I did when I was 20 years younger. This is especially true on religious issues!

Verse 29: I won't say that Khayyám beats this point to death, but he does repeat himself, though the point is well worth making.

Verse 30: Abbot and Costello made *Who's on First* part of a 1937 vaudeville routine on *Hollywood Bandwagon*.

Verse 31: Can you miss the reference to Star Trek? The original's references to the seventh gate and Saturn bring to mind the Ptolemaic theory of the spheres, where the earth is at the center of fixed domes that include the moon, Mercury, Venus, the Sun, Mars, Jupiter and Saturn. Ptolemy was a Greek mathematician, geographer, and astronomer, who used Babylonian observations and Babylonian lunar theory to develop his theory of the spheres. (See my note at verse 47, too.)

Verse 32: The door without a key will show up again in verse 55.

Verse 33: Blind trust can either be very liberating or very scary.

Verse 34: The crux of Omar's theology, and perhaps the crux of mine: God or fate may really be in control, but we must act based on the things we can experience. Enjoy life, do good, love with all your heart, dance, and sing. There may be more, but what if not? And if you believe and there is more, what is wrong with getting the most out of the life God has given you?

Verse 35: Back to the Eagles' *Hotel California*, though this time the song says, "Some *dance* to remember, some *dance* to forget." Others have said, "Some drink to remember, others drink to forget."  Jackie Gleason is quoted saying, "Some drink to forget, some drink to remember—me, I drink to get bagged."  Either way, alcohol is the catalyst.

Verse 36: When a good friend of ours died in 2008, I spoke at her funeral. She had undergone diabetes, kidney dialysis, cancer, and a failed transplant. It seemed like everything kept piling up on her, but she always presented a cheerful spirit. If "God is the Potter and we are the clay," this verse asks Him a pointed question. I have worked just a little with clay and understand thumping. You slam the wet clay over and over as hard as you can to get the air bubbles out. Sometimes you wonder if God could be a little gentler with us. The "obliterated tongue" reminds me of a Stephen Crane poem: "There was a man with tongue of wood who essayed to sing, And in truth it was lamentable. But there was one who heard the clip-clapper of this tongue of wood and knew what the man wished to sing, And with that the singer was content."

Verse 37: There is a deep discussion to yesterday, today and tomorrow in verse 47.

Verse 38: There are many good treatments to the theme that boils down our life to a single moment, whether it's the 2001 Moulin Rouge *Elephant Medley* ("Just one night, give me just one night … We could be heroes for just one day! … Love makes us act like we are fools, throw our lives away for one happy day.") or Trans-Siberian Orchestra's 2000 *Beethoven's Last Night*, with two songs: The *Dreams of Candlelight* ("Could this night it last forever … And we would live inside this night.") or *I'll Keep Your Secrets* ("And when the darkness starts to fall … Know at that moment I will be with you. I'll be around when there's no reason left to carry on.")  But the direct new reference is to Queen's *Who Wants to Live Forever* from 1986: ("There's no chance for us, It's all decided for us. The world has only one sweet moment set aside for us.")

Verse 39. Mac Davis came out with the song, *Stop and Smell the Roses*, in 1974.

Verse 40: We don't know if Khayyám was married. Some references say he had a wife and two children, some say he never married.

Verse 41: Stephen Crane again: "When the prophet, a complacent fat man, arrived at the mountain-top He cried: 'Woe to my knowledge! I intended to see good white lands and bad black lands—But the scene is grey.'"

Verse 42: In Fitzgerald's Rubáiyát, meet the "wine porter" who brings the kegs of wine into the tavern. He wears a heavy leather pad called a shoulder-knot to keep the keg straps from crippling him. Of course, to Khayyám, he's an angel. I often tell people that I am a better person after one gin and tonic, and certainly prefer that effect to the discord of the arguments in verses 24 to 30.

Verse 43: Though I was trained in debate and learned to argue fine points of theology, I stand with the crew from *Who's Line Is It, Anyway*, the improvisational radio and television show. The American version (1998 forward) reminds us that "it's all made up and the points don't matter."

Verse 44: I am reluctant to pin evil on any one religion or zealot, but certainly understand the fear of the unseen, relentless enemy represented by the "Dark Side" in Star

Wars or the Dementors of Azkaban in the Harry Potter series.

Verse 45: Another Stephen Crane poem reads, "If there is a witness to my little life, To my tiny throes and struggles, He sees a fool; and it is not fine for Gods to menace fools."

Verse 46: This allusion is the same, even as it changes over time. Consider Shakespeare's soliloquy from *As You Like It* (Act II, Scene VII): "All the world's a stage, and all the men and women merely players."

Verse 47: If our life is such a tiny component of the universe, it's easy to think that it is nothing. At the same time, it is everything. There is no difference between one second and a thousand years. 2 Peter 3:8 says, "do not forget this one thing, that with the Lord one day is as a thousand years, and a thousand years as one day."  Based on Einstein's Theory of Relativity, it can be said that the earth *is* the center of the universe—that the sun, moon, planets, stars, and galaxies all revolve around the earth in complex and contradictory paths. Everything that ever was or will be *is*. There is no difference in a thousand years and a split second. In fact, there is no difference in all the time since the big bang until the end of the universe. It exists, or it does not. The nature of consciousness is that from our perspective, we are the center of the universe, and this moment is the center of our time. When we die, we lose consciousness, but remain in every way a part of the universe that is.

Verse 48: We have lots of recent experience with hospice, and I can't help but think of the morphine they give near the end as the cocktail of death. Whether it's the hemlock of Socrates or the vinegar they gave to Jesus on the cross, the time comes for each of us to take the last drink.

Verse 49: I am a chess player, too. Khayyám repeatedly points out the transposition of the player and the played.

Verse 50: It was the *Original Amateur Hour* radio and television show (1934 through the 1960s) that really popularized the line: "Round and round she goes, and where she stops, nobody knows."  Whether fate or gambling or sports, from the right perspective, somebody knows where the ball is going.

Verse 51: Martin Luther King cited the original of this verse in his anti-war speech in 1967: "There is an invisible book of life that faithfully records our vigilance or our neglect. Omar Khayyam is right: 'The moving finger writes, and having writ moves on.'" Sam Ervin, the colorful North Carolina senator who presided over the Watergate hearings, incorrectly suggested in 1967 that Omar was wrong in the age of computers, that "not only do we lure it back, but cancel lines, alter them and wash them out completely, not with tears, but with the touch of a button."  In so saying, he proved the point he had made a few sentences earlier in the Congressional Record, describing his first day working construction just after he finished high school. "I was pushing a wheelbarrow and my boss asked what I was doing. I replied, 'They told me to carry dirt in this wheelbarrow.' The boss said, 'You put that thing down—you know you don't know anything about machinery.'"

Verse 52: Another reference, perhaps, to the spheres of Ptolemy, where it appears the earth is in the first "dome."

Verse 53: If God is omniscient, and can know every detail of the future, just as he knows every detail of the past, are we not just a book already written? The book won't change, we just haven't read the last chapter yet.

Verse 54: Khayyám and the Calvinists now take it farther and suggest that not only does God (or Fate) know the end of the story, but that the story is completely predestined—written in the stars. The flaming foal is the sun; Mushtara is Jupiter; and Parwín is the Pleiades constellation.

Verse 55: There is more alchemy in the original, the idea of turning a base metal into gold. Perhaps Khayyám can become the key from verse 32, unlocking the door to secrets that the Sufi mystics will never understand.

Verse 56: I have nothing against churches but find that most people in church are wearing a mask, putting up a façade. People are more genuine in a bar.

Verse 57: Predestination is advanced again. If God controls everything, how can we be blamed for anything—but even the blame is predetermined.

Verse 58: The new reference is from Daniel 5, where the Babylonian King Belshazzar is holding a feast, drinking from the captured Jewish sacred temple vessels. A hand appears writing on the wall: MENE, MENE, TEKEL, UPARSHIN. The king calls the prophet Daniel to interpret. Daniel explains, "Numbered, numbered, weighed, divided. The days of your kingdom are numbered and have come to an end. You have been weighed in the balance and are found lacking. Today your kingdom is taken from you and divided between the Medes and the Persians."

Verse 59: KUZA-NAMA is the book of Pots. The next 8 verses, through verse 66 are like a *Nutcracker* vision that will last until the end of Ramadan. The theme is consistent through many religions, even Christianity, where we sing, "Thou art the Potter, I am the Clay." (*Have Thine Own Way, Lord* by Adelaide Pollard, 1862 – 1934) Ramadan

(Ramazan) is the ninth month of the Islamic calendar, beginning with the sighting of one crescent moon and extending to the sighting of the next. Since it is a time of fasting and prayer (and often a lent-like abstinence), Khayyám looks forward to the "better moon" that signals the end of deprivation. To me, verse 36 belongs here as part of the book of pots, too.

Verse 60: In later editions of Fitzgerald's Rubáiyát, the first speaking pot becomes a Sufi pipkin (tiny pot), losing his temper. Perhaps this symbolizes less the philosophical question "Did God create man, or man create God," and more just the Sufi tendency to over-analyze the smallest activities.

Verse 61: If there is a God, and he gives us life, why would he want to take it away?

Verse 62: Not only did we take some work, but He developed a relationship with us that would make it hard to part.

Verses 63: Not all pots come out well, and some people are deformed either in body or spirit. If we are deficient, was there something intrinsic or based on our circumstance of life to blame?

Verse 64: The Tapster represents an innkeeper, pouring the wine for us. But is it God or is it the devil? In Fitzgerald's later edition it becomes: "'Why,' said another, 'Some there are who tell of one who threatens he will toss us to Hell. The luckless Pots he marred in making—Pish! He's a Good Fellow and 't will all be well.'"

Verse 65: Even the pots have grown weary of the disputes, as in the tavern in verse 30. I need another drink!

Verse 66: The porter's knot, again, from verse 42.

Verse 67: The old Irish drinking song, A Jug of Punch, was sung by AL Lloyd in 1956. "And when I'm dead and I'm in my grave no costly tombstone will I crave. Just lay me down in my native peat with a jug of punch at my head and feet."

Verse 68: Later, Fitzgerald made it clear that the wine of the vine-leaf wrap, or perhaps the wine-pickled body was the source of the sweet perfume, not just that fact that the ashes were buried in a garden.

Verse 69: Omar was apparently accused of being impious and strove to improve his reputation by going on a pilgrimage.

Verse 70: It is an interesting religious concept that it is ok to party to the max, then atone for it with some kind of penance, then do it all again.

Verse 71: In the house where I grew up, alcohol was absolutely forbidden. It was a gradual path that led me to appreciate the altered state brought on by just the perfect amount of gin. Too much, and you lose the creativity and energy you need to be productive, unless you're a Hemmingway.

Verse 72: Remember the nightingale, from verse 6? The circle of life comes to an end.

Verse 73: This one was circled by Jancie, perhaps in hope that the angst of our teen years could be turned into something that would truly make us both happy. We did not marry after high school but went our separate ways for more than ten years. We recently celebrated our 35th anniversary.

Verse 74: Early in our relationship, I wrote for Jancie: "You are the love of my life, and whether the paths of our lives may be joined in a cord of love, or if they be frayed in the wind, In the Annals of Heaven it will always be written, You are the love of my life."

Verse 75: I think this was the first Rubáiyát verse I actually used at a funeral, for Jancie's major professor, Dick Lee, who died after a stay with hospice. I had known him, too, as he and I had co-officiated the first wedding I performed. Later, I would bury my older brother, his wife, my father, and my mother in the same cemetery. When you imagine all the people buried there, and in all the graveyards in all the world, and realize that all the people that ever lived and ever will live wind up in a place like this, it should fill you not with despair, but with purpose, as it says in the song from *Les Misérables*, *I dreamed a Dream*: to leave no song unsung, no wine untasted.

# ACKNOWLEDGEMENTS

I was helped immensely by the notes on each of the verses maintained at:

www.bobforrestweb.co.uk/The_Rubaiyat/verse_by_verse_notes.htm


I am indebted to Collins Greetings Books and their edition of the Rubáiyát that Jancie gave me in 1969 which I used for reference in creating this work. Collins was founded in Glasgow in 1819 and merged with Harper & Row in 1990 to become HarperCollins.


Much of the work was done in seclusion with my wife and a good friend, Teresa Olson, at our house in Mississippi. Thanks for the support, suggestions, proofreading and encouragement.

# ABOUT THE AUTHOR

Jay Ter Louw is an Information Technology project manager and senior consultant in the health care industry. His father and grandfather were Reformed Church and Presbyterian ministers, and Jay was a lay minister, preaching for a Tallahassee retirement center for more than 20 years. He has performed dozens of weddings and funerals for people of all faiths.

Jay and Jancie met at Leon High School, class of 1969.

Comments are welcome, and may be sent to jayterlouw@gmail.com

www.ingramcontent.com/pod-product-compliance
Lightning Source LLC
Chambersburg PA
CBHW020509160726
47991CB00007B/2878